Inner Ha

Putting Your Self Back in Charge

Beth Rogerson, PhD

Printed in the United States of America

First Printing, 2015

ISBN-13: 978-0-692-46382-6

www.bethrogerson.com

Table of contents:

Introduction

The only journey is the one within. – Rainer Maria Rilke

I want to tell you about an experience I had as a young adult, before I learned about the Internal Family Systems model of self-coaching.

I walked into work one day and sat down at my desk and was hit with a wave of nostalgia, then melancholy. Sadness washed over me. I was not surfing this wave; I was deep in it, and I could not account for why it was there overpowering me.

Later that night when I was home, I sat quietly and reflected with curiosity on the day's events and sad emotions. Where had they come from?

I began to write in my journal (a critical component of self-coaching). Growing up, my family had moved about every three years from my infancy until I was 13. Every three years I said goodbye to all the friends I had made, routines, and familiar places and then moved to another home and school where I would need to make new friends and routines.

And every time there was a move, my mother got the new home ready by cleaning and painting the interior.

That was it! My office had been painted over the weekend and the lingering smell of the paint triggered the sadness and loss from my early life. As I recognized and named this sadness, I felt it release its hold on me.

I realized I was in the car of life. But I was in the back seat with a toy wheel, very sure I was in control. When I found the Internal Family Systems (IFS) model, I knew it was finally time to ride up front in Self Leadership.

What is Internal Family Systems (IFS)?

The way to climb out of the back seat of the car and get into the driver's seat is to get to know your inner world. At earlier points in your life this may have seemed too dangerous, too scary, or maybe even silly.

This time will be different because you will have the IFS framework to guide you. Quite simply, IFS describes your inner world as being like a family. Think of your own family. It's probably safe to say you don't always get along with each other. When this happens inside you, you can fall into eating, drinking, or shopping too much, or any of those other excessive quick fixes that don't actually fix anything at all.

This book will give you the actionable tips you need to tap into your inner calm, compassion, and curiosity to handle any emotional challenge that comes your way. You'll gain greater confidence and build stronger relationships with your loved ones as you get to know your inner family over time.

Those words of negativity
That often times can fill my heart
Are coming from a part of me
It is from this place I start
To turn now with curiosity
To question, not to blame
For before I saw my parts
I viewed my whole Self as the same
Not sunshine and storm clouds
But just a cloudy sky of grey
And with my curious attention
Now the storm clouds float away
And my parts become a rainbow
All the colors from within
Deep comfort and compassion
From the Self that lives within

– Denise Conway

How to Use this Book

Here are some tips for getting the most out of this book.

1. **Begin a practice of journaling while you read.** You don't need a fancy notebook to do this work. A plain old notepad will do.
2. **Write down any discoveries you make as you read, and note your thoughts at the end of each chapter.** You'll be surprised how much your inner world has to say once you're really listening.
3. **Don't worry if you need to refer often to earlier parts of this book.** As you come to understand how IFS works, it will get easier to do. Your journal can help you here, too.
4. **Approach this book as you would any lifestyle change.** Imagine you wanted to eat healthier. You'd make changes to how you shop at the grocery store and change the kinds of foods you eat. As you do this IFS work, you will prepare an environment where you can take care of your mind and your emotions.
5. **Remember, you don't have to go it alone.** I wrote this book because I believe you can begin this work on your own, but, this is not easy work. If you need support from a trained and certified IFS therapist, I recommend visiting www.selfleadership.org.

Get Out Your Journal: Now is a good time to write down what you hope IFS will do for you. What made you decide to take this journey? What are you hoping will be different in your life?

Chapter 1
An Overview of the Internal Family Systems Model (IFS)

Trust yourself. Create the kind of self that you will be happy to live with all your life. Make the most of yourself by fanning the tiny, inner sparks of possibility into flames of achievement. – Golda Meir

The Internal Family Systems (IFS) model, developed by Richard C. Schwartz, Ph.D. (1995), provides a lens for self-understanding that's unlike other things you've probably tried. When you put your IFS goggles on and look at your inner world, you'll learn to see that you are made up of your:

- Self
- Parts

IFS sees the Core Self and parts as the family inside of you (when referring to your Core Self, the word Self will be capitalized). But a more helpful metaphor is to think of the **Self** as the conductor for the orchestra of your mind, and the **parts** are the talented experienced musicians. When the Self is in charge of the parts, you have harmony.

Disharmony happens to all of us. How is it that the band falls out of tune? In his book *Incognito: The Secret Lives of the Brain*, neuroscientist David Eagleman suggests a slightly different analogy: our brains are made up of conflicting parts, like a jury of peers in a courtroom trial. Here we have the twelve strangers who work together in collaboration and in conflict to arrive at a single decision.

When we say, *a part of me wants to take this new job and move to Los Angeles, but a part of me wants to stay here and be near my family and friends*, what we are speaking reflects what the neuroscientists are stating. There are, in fact, different active parts of our brain with different wants and needs!

In other words, our brains have competing sub-personalities, or subsystems. These are the parts. This is where IFS gets its name. Like in families, there are different parts that parent, criticize, react, align, and fall into conflict.

I must emphasize, **your parts have good intentions for you**. Over the years they have helped you many times. Our goal is not to get rid of any of the parts, even if they're difficult! Rather, the goal is to bring them all back into harmony and resolve the inner conflict.

Many believe we are born into harmony. Even before we are born, however, we meet events in our lives that disrupt and require adaptation. Research supports how a mother's external life will make changes to her unborn child, causing parts to come into being. Simply put, as we adapt to meet the demands of our environment, we create coping mechanisms which become parts of us. Most of our parts are developed before we reach 18 years old.

Our Changing Brains

The brain is a far more open system than we ever imagined, and nature has gone very far to help us perceive and take in the world around us. It has given us a brain that survives in a changing world by changing itself.
– Norman Doidge, M.D.

We may not be born into harmony, but because of our Self qualities, we are born with the ability to lead a harmonious life. And it's never too late to start. The last fifteen years of neuroscientific research have effectively disproved the old adage *you can't teach an old dog new tricks.*

Previous thinking about brain development had us all convinced that once we reached adulthood, our brains were fixed in place like a prehistoric mosquito in amber, end of story.

That's simply not so. Through experiments and research in the field of neuroplasticity, the study of how our brains change, we know now that the brain is **plastic** and can in fact be changed.

Neuroplastician Alvaro Pascual-Leone, M.D., Ph.D., conducted an experiment to test if the brain itself changes merely as a result of the thoughts we think.

One group of people physically learned how to do an activity, and the second group merely visualized learning to do it. *The visualizing group learned the activity just as accurately as the practicing group, which indicates our thoughts alone can cause changes in the brain.*

Just thinking about playing a tune on the piano leads to measurable changes in the brain's motor cortex (Begley).

Psychiatrist and psychoanalyst Norman Doidge, M.D., shares in his book *The Brain that Changes Itself* shocking yet inspiring stories about the power of thoughts. With training, stroke patients regain their abilities and people erase their lifelong depression and anxiety. Thoughts even switch certain genes on and off, according to Doidge.

In short, there is clear evidence that we can change our brains and be happier.

Get Out Your Journal: Are you convinced old dogs can learn new tricks? Think about a change you want to make in your life. What are some things you might need to look at? What are some things you can do in the present to make that change happen?

Chapter 2
Who Are These Parts, and Where Did They Come From?

Parts are forced into extreme roles by external circumstances and, once it seems safe, they gladly transform into valuable [internal] family members. – Richard C. Schwartz, Ph.D.

The easiest way to understand the idea of "parts" is to think of them like little people inside of you. They have their own needs, wants, and agendas, and they interact with each other just the way people interact.

An example of being in a part (as opposed to being in Self) is when you feel angry. Imagine this scenario:

- Your boss has asked you to stay late to work on the very night you really wanted to go home and have dinner with your family.
- When you do get home, the dog won't stop barking, your child keeps asking to play, and your partner hasn't even started dinner.
- You're also hungry.

Is it really any surprise when you explode with anger? Perhaps it may feel like you had no choice but to react this way. So maybe it's not a surprise, but do you really enjoy feeling that angry and dealing with the aftermath?

This doesn't have to happen to you. And by "this" I mean have a part go extreme on you. **Understanding your parts is the first step in leading from Self.**

Why do parts become extreme in their current roles?

- **We have extreme events in our lives.** Divorce, moving, the loss of a loved one, and having to work late every day and miss dinner with your family are a few examples of extreme life events.
- **We are taking poor care of ourselves.** Staying up too late too frequently, spending too much time with our beloved screens, drinking too much alcohol or taking care of others instead of ourselves for too long.

Whether the stress comes from outside of us, or from inside of ourselves, the result is the same. When you're stressed:

- Your **manager** parts go into overdrive until they are too tired to do more.
- Then the doors are open and your **exile** parts burst out.
- Then your **firefighter** parts run in to put out the emotional fire. They do this by pleasing and distracting you with excessive shopping, binge eating, drinking alcohol, and such. They throw as much of these as you need to put out the fire.

And *nobody* - managers, exiles, firefighters, and especially you - is happy with the mess that's left.

Who *are* these managers, exiles, and firefighters, seemingly causing all this chaos? I'll explain shortly, but first let's find out where these little people came from.

Where did these parts come from?

Were you parents more likely to smile at you and hug you when you followed the rules in your home, growing up? You probably learned quickly the link between "being good" and feeling nurtured and valued.

As a result, you may have a subconscious belief that *if I am good and do what others need and want, they will value me and I will feel safe.* A part is formed that wants very much to please others. That's not a bad part to have. But when it goes into overdrive, you can become resentful and unhappy that others take away so much from you.

We are biologically programmed to develop survival and adaptive behaviors to meet the challenges of being alive. When we repeat these behaviors over and over, the neurons in our brains fire over and over again, and over time, we wire a pattern of behavior. We create a **pathway** in our brain (neural networks) that **supports** this way of behaving or coping.

Around this behavior, a part is formed.

Parts fall into two categories:

- Exiles
- Protectors

The protector parts are **managers** and **firefighters**.

Exiled Parts

Our exiled parts formed in response to pain and distress during our childhoods. Exiles hold old, outdated beliefs formed during these difficult, or even traumatic, times in our young lives. They are our sensitive areas that hold our emotional pain and when they are triggered, we feel hurt.

Exiles show up in our present lives when we find ourselves in situations that mirror those early difficult experiences. We can be completely blown off course by these deep feelings, and we hear ourselves repeat those beliefs. *I am not worthy. I am unlovable. I will never be valued because I am bad.*

When exiles show up holding all that emotional pain from all those difficult, maybe even traumatic times, chaos follows in their wake. Just like in the example about staying late at work.

The part of you that needed to be a good and valued employee may have taken over when your boss asked you to stay late. That part went into overdrive, not paying attention to the needs of the other parts of you, leaving you exhausted and in need of calm, attention, and care. The barking dog, demanding child, and unhelpful partner stand in your way to fulfilling your needs.

In response, you lead with your angry part that outwardly seems disproportionate to the actual situation. Your angry part attempts to push all this noise away from you to create the quiet space you want.

Also, you may be experiencing an exiled part of you that did not feel valued and cared for at a younger age, and holds sadness and feelings of being ignored. This present experience is igniting these deeply sad feelings.

Rather than let you become overwhelmed with these sad emotions, your anger comes in quickly to take up the emotional space inside of you. In this moment, you are angry, not sad. The anger passes and your manager parts come in to make amends and clean up any problems the anger may have caused. The sadness is gone, exiled from your consciousness.

These are the Firefighters.

Protectors: Firefighter Parts

Firefighters are a type of protector part. Your firefighter parts respond to emotional emergencies, rushing in to keep negative emotions from overwhelming you.

Firefighters manifest themselves in coping behaviors, aka, your favorite soothing pastimes done in excess. Eating, shopping, drinking alcohol, sleeping, surfing the internet, or couch potato-ing. Anger itself can be a firefighter. Instead of feeling the sadness from a triggered, exiled part, you get angry - fast and loud.

Parts that act as firefighters are rushing in to put out the pain from the emotions held by your exiled parts in any way that works fast.

These self-distractions or other extreme emotions that flood in provide immediate emotional relief in your Self system. But the manager parts have to clean up the mess from the firefighters, and managers don't like damage control. The relief disappears as the managers go into overdrive needing to organize, work hard, criticize, and get everything back in shape.

The internal family system could be more at ease if it could get to know the exiles and welcome them to return. Then there would not be these surprises and extreme reactions.

Managers are the other type of protector part. Managers manage our everyday lives, thoughts, and behaviors to keep us safe emotionally both inside and outside of ourselves. Managers make sure we look "good" on the outside by striving, planning, judging, and criticizing.

Often unknown to you, your manager parts have built a system of being and interacting so the exiles will not come out and overwhelm you in your everyday life.

Managers are the parts we formed to help us cope with difficult times. Some examples of managers and their origins are:

- **Perfectionism:** This may have grown in reaction to difficult and neglectful parenting.

- **A beautiful, well-developed imagination:** This may be an adaptation to growing up in an abusive home.
- **A reputation of reliability in getting the job done and following the rules:** This may have come from having to step up and take on the responsibilities of an alcoholic parent.

Think of the boss who asked you to stay late. This manager part prioritized looking good at work over having dinner with your family because that's what was good for you at work. See how this choice was made without considering how other parts of you felt about that decision?

On the other hand, we develop parts even if we view our early lives as unblemished by trauma and tragedy. Think of a colicky baby whose parents care for him or her lovingly and gently, but whose experience is still one of fear and pain. No one can stop the pain, and even as a baby he or she comes to view the world as unsafe. The baby may even feel abandoned.

To survive, this infant may form a part that wants to be in charge at all times because he or she has experienced the world as unsafe, and from that experience has formed a belief: *no one is here to help me*. Sadly, the baby's parent may see him or her as a willful, difficult child, and react to the child with one of their parts, and then the dance begins.

You Can Transform your Exiled Parts

Your exiled parts behave this way because your protector parts have exiled them from your internal family system. This makes sense because your experience of your exiles is that they make you extremely unhappy! The protectors are just trying to shield you from the emotional pain the exiles hold, even if it creates more difficulties for you down the road.

The solution is to bring the exiles back into the family. You may have tried this before but decided "never again!" because of the pain it brought you.

It will work this time because in chapters 4, 5, and 6 you will learn how to build trust between your protectors and your exiles. As your protector parts begin to know the calm, compassion, and curiosity of Self, they begin to relax in their roles of protection. They no longer are worried about the exiles overrunning your system.

This trust brings down the inside wall and begins the return of the exiles to your internal system. Your Self can see, hear, and acknowledge the earlier stories your exiles hold. You can get to know their beliefs and help to update them with new information. The calm and compassion that you bring to these conversations give your protectors and exiles freedom to make different choices.

In short, the band starts to fall back in tune. The key to harmony is the calm, compassion, and curiosity only the Self can bring.

Get Out Your Journal: What are your usual firefighter parts that show up when you are feeling a wave of negative emotions?

Chapter 3
The Self

We have all a better guide in ourselves, if we would attend to it, than any other person can be. – Jane Austen

We fall into disharmony in our lives when the Self is not conducting the orchestra of our parts. Self is always present but it gets usurped by different parts of us trying to "do" or "be" what those parts think is best for us. Getting back to being in Self - as opposed to being in a part - requires understanding Self and its qualities.

I can best explain Self by describing to you my own personal quest for Self leadership. It began at the end of an IFS therapy training. I struck up a casual conversation with Richard Schwartz, innovator of the IFS model. With concern, compassion, and calm he answered all of my questions when he said, "As long as you stay with Self, your life will unfold as it needs."

But then he said the playful words that struck me like lightning: "May the Self be with you!" *All at once, I knew what I needed to do.* I had to get more Self. I had to discover this Self within me.

On my journey, I met many of my parts. At times, I felt that I was *only* parts, that there was no Self in me to know. Meeting my parts was an important part of the process, but I was going about getting more Self the wrong way.

Instead of focusing so much on the abstract nature of Self, I needed to practice Self qualities. Self within us is always present. As we experience the qualities that Self embodies, we can begin to uncover and bring more of Self into our lives. When we are present in this Self energy we feel more in balance with our parts and more connected with ourselves and others.

The eight **qualities** of Self are:

- Calm
- Compassion
- Curiosity
- Clarity
- Creativity
- Connection
- Courage
- Confidence

This book focuses on the first three Self qualities and how you can develop them deeper.

The more Self energy we generate, the more ability we have to connect with our parts. Our parts begin to trust us to lead with this Self energy. In turn, the more predominant Core Self calls upon the abilities of our different parts to advise a solution that's best for everyone in our internal system.

Daniel Goleman wrote about **emotional intelligence** in *Emotional Intelligence: Why it Can Matter More Than IQ*. He said having emotional intelligence is the ability to monitor your own emotions and to skillfully use this information to guide your thinking and actions. Through the IFS lens, we see the close relationship between emotional intelligence and Self.

Self Quality #1: Calm

Calm is the starting place for Self. When you are calm, you have the space to observe and be curious toward what is happening inside of you. Calm gives you the inner spaciousness to do more than anxiously attend to what is happening outside of you.

A feeling of calm peacefulness floods our bodies when we are at rest.

We can bring this calm into our bodies through changing our breath, guiding our imagery, and welcoming our thoughts and emotions as messengers to guide us toward wisdom and right action.

Self Quality #2: Compassion

Having Self compassion is turning our empathy, warmth, and caring inward toward our own emotional pain. We intentionally extend kindness to ourselves, much in the way we would toward a friend who was hurting. The friend feels your caring and focused attention and begins to calm down and feel better. It's important to do this for yourself, too.

Pain happens to all humanity; suffering our pain is more of a choice. We can choose how we react to pain. Compassion allows us to begin to change the way we relate to our thoughts and emotions. We can't change the events of our past, but with compassion we change our relationship to it. We can offer ourselves comfort which allows trust to grow in our inner system.

Calm, curiosity, and compassion brings better relating with ourselves, others, and our world. In the next three chapters, we'll learn how to exercise these Self qualities.

Get Out Your Journal: Reflect on the Self quality of compassion and write down a time you remember befriending yourself. As you remember this, how do you feel?

Self Quality #3: Curiosity

When we are mindful and calm, we can invite curiosity and wonderment. This is known as "beginner's mind." We feel an open, nonjudgmental, and caring curiosity toward ourselves. In this place, there is no need to make meaning of the sensations and emotions flowing from our rational, logical mind. Instead, we observe ourselves having an emotion and ask: *What is this emotion? What does it want me to know?*

This mind shift is significant. We go from thinking we are that emotion to understanding it is merely a part of us.

Being mindful and choosing to extend curiosity and nonjudgmental observing is a skill you can learn and practice. At first, this mindful noticing doesn't feel there at all, then it is awkwardly there, and then it is quietly always present. The more you use it, the more natural it feels. Wake up in your life. Get Curious.

Chapter 4
Cultivating Calm

You are the sky. Everything else – it's just the weather. – Pema Chödrön

Calm is the starting place for Self. When you are calm, you not only feel relaxed, but you also experience something I call "inner spaciousness." Calm makes room for you to observe and be curious about what is happening inside of you. This feeling of inner spaciousness allows you to clearly take in information from both inside and outside of you. You have access to more possibilities to guide you in your choices.

What happens when we are not calm? We can get caught up in anxiously attending to what is happening outside of us, which is not bad, necessarily. It's a survival mechanism from our caveman days. We step into this flight-fight-freeze response in reaction to danger, real or perceived. It happens in our minds and our bodies. We sense emotional or physical danger and it triggers both a physical and emotional reaction.

Stress, as we so fondly name this response, simply means:

- We have gotten stuck in this naturally-programed survival mechanism.
- So, we make decisions out of a hyper-aroused state, and not from calm responding.
- We are not connected to what we need and want: we are in an automatic response.

We don't have to remain stuck. Thankfully our brain has developed more since caveman times! We have other options. We can connect to a different part of our brain, the executive function, and:

- Move quickly through the flight-fight-freeze response
- Take a step back and observe what is happening, predict what will happen next, and respond to the situation calmly and objectively
- Detach from the moment and use our thoughts, feelings, and emotions to respond in a better way

This being in another part of our brain while experiencing a stressful situation is a form of being mindful.

We can unstick ourselves in one of two ways. According to trauma expert Bessel van der Kolk, M.D., we can approach this from the top down or bottom up.

- **Top down** takes place through mindfulness and using the more "advanced" part of our brain.
- **Bottom up** uses the least advanced, or primitive, brain. It's often referred to as the reptilian brain. We tap into our reptilian brain through using our breath to bring calm into our bodies.

Both approaches are important.
Next, we'll learn how to use them.

Practicing Calm from the Bottom Up

We are built to feel and respond to stress, but we are also built to relax and recuperate. We become out of balance just because of the on-the-go kind of lives we live.

We can reset ourselves and bring calm to our system through **breath**. Breath is an important part of bringing in calm presence.

Our breath is both something we do whether we ignore it or pay attention to it. When we change our breath, it then changes how we think and feel. That is pretty awesome!

Breath work is the practice of becoming conscious of your breath and then regulating your breath. It puts you in charge of bringing in calm. Full, deep breathing slows down our breath and signals to the brain "no danger present!" This activates the part of our nervous system that brings rest and calm to our overall system.

Breathing Exercise #1: Observing Your Breath

If you've ever practiced yoga or meditation, this exercise will be familiar to you. I encourage you to start with this exercise right here, right now, no matter what your level of experience. It will ground you in the work to come.

1. Breathe in and out through your nose. Breathing through your nose naturally deepens your breath. Direct yourself to observe from a neutral, or nonjudgmental, place of wondering. Just notice what is happening as you follow this exercise.
2. Observe your natural way of breathing. Do this by closing your eyes and directing your awareness inward. Don't try to change how you're breathing. Notice how your awareness begins to focus on what is inside.
3. Breathe deeper so you can feel your abdomen expanding as your lungs fill.
4. Count your natural breath. How many breaths out? How many breaths in? Do this for a few minutes so you can know your natural breath. This is your base line for now. This is what has become a habitual way of breathing for you. There is no judgment, just you noticing.
5. Now breathe so your exhale is twice as long as your inhale. This is called 1:2 breathing.
6. When you're done, journal what you noticed about yourself during this exercise. What sensations, thoughts, emotions? Anything different?

Notice how you're feeling after that? That's the feeling of having more Self, in the form of calm, available to you. You can just "be" with your parts, or be more connected to others in relationships when this calm is present.

The exhale activates the parasympathetic nervous system and slows us down for rest and digesting. Breathing this way will slow down your heart rate and make room for calm. This type of breathing helps release neurochemicals that support the mind worrying less, which reduces your anxiety.

Breathing Exercise #2: Being with Worry

In this breathing exercise you will use your breath to get a worrying part to move into the background.

1. Close your eyes and think of something that worries you. Let your thoughts unfold as they want around this worry.
2. Breathe deeply, through your nostrils.
3. Change to 1:2 breathing. Gradually lengthen your exhale to even longer. See how this feels. Let your exhale become twice as long as your inhale. If you breathe in for 3, then exhale for 6.
4. Continue breathing this way for 3-5 minutes.
5. Notice any calm sensations you are having, such as fewer thoughts, slower heartbeat, etc.
6. Journal whatever you experienced. For example, was this difficult or natural? Can you feel a different sensation between worried and calm? Do they feel separate or not?
7. Then revisit your worry and see if anything is different.

When you feel comfortable with this 1:2 breathing practice (where your exhale is twice as long as your inhale), you are ready to meet your worried part. With your eyes closed, imagine extending your calm breathing toward this part. In this calm, spacious awareness, you can notice your worried part and be curious about what it might need or want. You are calm in your breathing and noticing a worried part, both at the same time.

Later we will explore how to interview this part and get to know it better from qualities of Self.

Get Out Your Journal: Both breathing exercises asked you to journal, but now is a good time to reflect on the entire experience. Did you feel more calm coming from Self, even as you read the chapter? Do you feel more confident about meeting your parts? How do you feel about meeting your worried part? How did that go for you?

Chapter 5
Self Compassion

If I am not good to myself how can I expect anyone else to be good to me? – Maya Angelou

Think of how you feel when you sit with a good friend when you're feeling bad. As they listen to you, you feel held and cared for by them. You feel their empathy.

You can, and need to be, that good, empathetic friend to yourself. Self compassion is a tool for dealing with difficult emotions, and it's always available to us. Compassion opens the doors to change and personal growth as we get to know the parts that advise us as we lead our lives. Self compassion brings in calm and centered feelings as we begin to see a broader landscape inside ourselves, and this opens the way to more possibilities.

Many of us neglect Self compassion in favor of a critical part of ourselves when we are disappointed. We can be so accustomed to leading with a critical part that it can feel safe and familiar to us! If we don't hear that critical, judging voice toward ourselves all the time, we could feel anxious.

But in reality, having a loud critic in our head without really being aware of it makes us feel worse. Becoming aware of your critic and hearing what it wants you to know is important. And bringing Self compassion to yourself for how hard it is to be disappointed is necessary to keep your equilibrium. Since leading with a critic part is often an automatic response to a disappointment, it is the Self compassion that is less familiar to most of us and needs to be practiced and used intentionally.

When our internal critic gets too big and powerful, it can act like a bully. As a result, we don't fully get to express ourselves in our lives and we may feel unhappy or unfulfilled. This bully part may be tough on us, but, many times it has helped us get the job done. This is what makes it so hard to stop being so critical (see, there really are no bad parts, only ones that become extreme in our internal world!).

Bringing Self compassion to your internal world can relax your extreme parts and help them step down and not work so hard.

The Science of Self Compassion

The research on Self compassion is new and growing. What it suggests is that people who are Self compassionate:

- Tend to experience fewer negative emotions overall
- Have greater emotional intelligence (meaning they are better able to maintain emotional balance in the face of difficult circumstances)
- Have a lower level of the stress hormone cortisol because they are more Self compassionate than self critical

The stress and non-stop nature of our lives can frequently kick off our flight-fight-freeze response, making us less effective at achieving results. Feelings of disappointment and failure can flood us. We attack ourselves and stimulate certain pathways in our brain that attack and blame inward but most likely outward (more stress and high alert!).

What is underdeveloped is our ability to respond instead with inner support and caring. This type of response activates the side of our nervous system that allows us to relax and take in the new information that could actually benefit us at this time.

Five Steps to Becoming Self Compassionate

Does all of this sound awkward to you? What if I told you practicing Self compassion meant you could learn from your critic part, instead of just feeling bad? Self compassion removes the emotionally painful impacts of the criticism and makes way for discovery.

Here are 5 necessary components for easing into Self compassion:

1. Have the courage to embrace compassion and not see it as something that will weaken you and make you feel complacent. Have the courage to engage Self compassion over your critical voice.
2. Mindfully befriend yourself. You can extend the empathy you feel for others toward yourself. Just like you would listen to a good friend, you can also listen to your inner dialogue with observation and compassion. Befriend your parts that are triggered.
3. From a place of Self calm, allow yourself to be present with the different painful feelings you are experiencing in a gentle and caring way. Become open to exploring the feelings behind the criticism, and soon you will have the room to be curious about the information behind the self criticism. Allow your parts to come in and be open to what they are expressing
4. Set aside criticism and hurt and instead turn sympathy and caring toward yourself as you understand more about how hard this is for you right now. When we feel cared for, we are calmer. When we are calmer, we can see the bigger picture and have more solutions to whatever confronts us. Turn caring toward these parts of you and express how hard this is for you right now.
5. Notice how as you continue to extend kindness and tolerance to yourself, you experience an openness and belonging. You are a human being with a full range of emotions. You are not perfect, just like the other humans you know. This is Self acceptance.

You may not realize it, but when you practice Self compassion, you're building greater trust in your internal system. You feel safe in your life and free to make better choices for yourself.

Three Daily Practices for Self Compassion

Practicing Self compassion begins with **intentionality**. We set an intention to practice this underdeveloped skill.

The following exercises, done intentionally and practiced daily, will strengthen the neural network that ignites compassion in your brain. Over time, it will become effortless for you to extend compassion to yourself and the world around you (Neff).

1. You intentionally give yourself kindness and care, despite that fact it might feel unfamiliar or even fake. It will feel more familiar and natural the more you continue to practice it and strengthen neural networks.
2. You remind yourself that you are part of a greater human experience where pain is something all human beings experience. You are not alone.
3. You take a mindful approach to noticing your thoughts and emotions. When they arise you allow and welcome these feelings and parts. You recognize how they have information to share with you about what's happening. When you can see them as separate from you, then you can name them as parts and get to know them better.

Getting Started with Self Compassion

We can practice Self compassion as Self maintenance. We call this "daily kindness inside."

You'll want to have your journal out for this part. Self compassion shows up - or doesn't - in the language you use with yourself. You want to begin daily nonviolent communication with yourself.

1. Notice the language you use with yourself during your day. If you take a wrong turn while you're driving, do you hear yourself say *that was stupid?* Do you complete a project right on the deadline and say to yourself *too bad you didn't get it done sooner?*

2. What are other examples of how you talk to yourself like this? Write them down here.
3. Look at your examples. What do you notice? Calling yourself stupid for a mistake or pointing out something you could have done better may not seem so bad.
4. Now imagine your partner or friend is sitting next to you in the car when you take the wrong turn, and they say, "That was stupid." Do you find yourself reacting differently?
5. Look through your examples and pay attention to how you imagine you would feel if someone else said those things to you. Write those feelings down. (My guess is that it's not great).
6. Put yourself back in the car example. This time, take the wrong turn and say instead *Great recovery!* when you do a U-turn and find the perfect parking place.
7. From a place of calm, look at your examples again. Do you begin to see how you could say something nicer to yourself?

You can choose to use empathetic language with yourself instead of the judgmental language you've been using.

1. Remember that friend who was in a bad place? You listened to your friend and felt his or her pain. **Be that friend to yourself.**
2. Think of one of your examples. Say to yourself, *I'm sorry it is so hard right now. It is difficult. It makes sense you are feeling so sad.*
3. In the car example, imagine saying to yourself, *It makes sense that you would be frustrated when that happens. It's ok because you can make a U-turn right up there.*

Practicing peace with yourself means being kind and caring inside your head and heart. When you are kind to yourself and at peace with yourself, a great thing happens. You can respond to your life with more peace and less reactive actions. Peace begins with ourselves and then extends out into the world.

Below is a small practice designed from the work developed by Marshall Rosenberg, innovator and author of *Nonviolent Communication: A Language of Life*. Ask yourself and your parts these questions and listen as you would to a friend or a small child.

- What part is up in me right now?
- What feelings does this part of me hold?
- What information does this part give me about what I need?
- Is there some action I can take in my life in response to this part of me?

Listen to the answers with a friendly welcoming intention. Journal your responses.

Practicing Self Compassion in the Moment

When you find yourself flooded with negative feelings, thoughts, and judgments, one or more strong parts have been triggered in real time. Right now! What can you do?

First: Breathe deeper, go inside and breathe in calm. Be aware of being calm as you notice what is also happening on the outside. Slow down. Remember your intention is to **respond, not react.**

Get grounded in the present by breathing more deeply. Ground yourself in your breath by watching your breath, counting your breaths, and feeling yourself in your body.

Extend some curiosity to these feelings, thoughts, sensations. If this is difficult for you, take a timeout by leaving the situation or comforting yourself in the moment inside your head. When you can access your journal, write from your critical or triggered part.

Name the feeling, thought, sensation that is behind the criticism:

- "I did it wrong"
- "I am so stupid"
- "Now I have ruined everything"

All of these criticisms are associated with feelings of anger, disappointment, sadness, fear, or loneliness.

Second: Notice these feelings as sensations in your body. What do they feel like? Where are these sensations located? Around your heart? In your gut?

Imagine this in your body: what would it look like? Where is it?

Now send your Self compassion for the pain this thought/feeling/sensation is causing you both emotionally and physically.

Be Self compassionate by reminding yourself you are friends. Acknowledge how hard it is for you right now. Feel empathy for the hardship and painful feelings. Extend this caring and empathy toward yourself.

Continue to breathe deeply and fully (it may be helpful to follow the breathing exercises in Chapter Four before interviewing this part of yourself). As you notice the feelings of emotional pain, intentionally send caring kindness to yourself. A mantra can help. Kristen Neff, Ph.D., the leading researcher currently on Self compassion suggests this mantra:

> *This is a moment of suffering.*
> *Suffering is a part of life.*
> *May I be kind to myself in this moment.*
> *May I give myself the compassion I need.*

When it is difficult to speak kindly to yourself in your mind, a mantra is helpful. It is a memorized saying that you can repeat over and over to yourself until you feel calmer.

Third: Notice the spacious awareness created through your breath as you intentionally turn inward. There is space between the observing, caring you and the part of you that holds the emotions. This spaciousness is calm, not pressure. When you have this spaciousness, these feelings are held by you and will not overwhelm you.

When you can observe these sensations and feelings and feel calm, compassion, and curiosity, you are not just the unfolding feeling, thought, or sensations any longer but also a separate aware and caring Self. In this spacious place of calm awareness, you are unblended from the loud emotional parts of yourself. When you observe from kindness, calm, curiosity, and welcoming, you are stepping into your field of Self energy and all these "C" qualities it holds: calm, compassion, curiosity, clarity, creativity, connection, courage, and confidence. From this place, you meet your strong parts, who are messengers about what you need and want.

You will bring calm and peace internally with this practice. When you do, you will lead from this place in your life.

This is a difficult practice to do in real time. You can also practice it by sitting quietly, breathing, and remembering a time when you felt like the above. It will trigger the difficult emotions.

Get Out Your Journal: Journal by asking the above questions and writing from each part triggered.

Chapter 6
Self Curiosity

Between stimulus and response there is a space. In that space is our power to choose our response. In our response lies our growth and our freedom. – Viktor Frankl, M.D., Ph.D.

In the last two chapters you learned how to develop Self calm and Self compassion. Those Self energies create the right space to extend curiosity to yourself and to your parts. You have already started on the path of Self curiosity when you interviewed a part of yourself in the previous chapter. Now let's go deeper.

Curiosity is a strong desire to **know**. Why be curious about ourselves? What is the value?

Self curiosity is open, nonjudgmental, and caring. It is a relaxed yet aware state of being in Self-inquiry. As our Self and our parts experience this nonjudgmental openness, we begin a process that restores our understanding of who we really are in totality. This inward journey really is a new frontier and way of being with yourself.

Self curiosity is a wonderful way to understand ourselves more deeply. We can see the thoughts, beliefs, and emotions that gave rise to our parts. In some cases, we have over-identified with these parts of ourselves to the extent we believe we are that part. We call this being blended with a part. We may say something like *I am an organized person. I am a person who sees worse case scenarios. I plan things. I am a giving person.*

Notice how these statements sound like good things to be? And yet these are the thoughts and beliefs that can grow so big in us they become a trap. They create an inner glass ceiling that thwarts us from being in our life's purpose.

As we continue our journey inward, we continue to discover older, more difficult beliefs and emotions that we have held our whole lives. Now we can ask our parts *Are they really true?* Our parts experience the calm and compassion of Self and they begin to unknot and lose their emotional charge. We begin to befriend our parts instead of pushing them away.

Self curiosity is not only a backward-looking practice. It is also forward-looking in that we can apply it as emotions are happening to us in real time. In this place, there is no need for our rational mind to make meaning of the sensations and emotions we are experiencing. Instead, we observe ourselves having an emotion and ask *What is this emotion? What does it want me to know?*

The benefit of this awareness is that we start to have **choices**. We can choose where to direct our attention and how to respond to thoughts and feelings. Rather than identify with an emotion *I am angry,* we can instead recognize *A part of me holds anger right now* or *I feel like I am becoming blended or hijacked by anger*. We are able to **witness and connect** with our sensations, thoughts, and feelings, and not just react.

Practicing Self Curiosity, or Mindfulness

Practicing Self curiosity is really the practice of mindfulness. A mindfulness tool is the practice of noticing. We can understand mindfulness by looking at its practice:

1. **Stop** and notice what is happening and what you are doing. Slowing down what you are doing can support being mindful.
2. You stop as you are participating in your life and **observe** and note what is happening to yourself. Name your emotions - anger, sadness - and feel how they feel in your body.
3. If you get distracted, just return your attention to the sensation in your body and **inquire**. What is it telling you?

Note: Don't worry if you can't do this right in the exact moment something is happening to you. That takes practice. It's equally valuable to return to a difficult moment in reflection.

It may seem counterintuitive to pull a difficult emotion closer. But, how well has it worked to push it away? More often than not, it leads to an even stronger emotion that leads to a reactive response. The result is that we usually do not get what we need.

An example of this is when we have been busy doing many things for others and begin to sense we are unhappy. We're not getting our physical comforts or emotional needs met by Self or by others, and push the feeling back so we don't create (imagined) conflict. In response, we feel an even stronger emotion (anger) until we act on it. Our angry response pushes others away when what we need is for them to come closer and care for us. We feel regret and an even deeper unhappiness.

If the behavior becomes a pattern, we get trapped in a cycle we aren't aware of, but continue to choose anyway!

We can step outside the storyline when we practice mindfulness. We can **feel** the hurt and anger, but we do not **become** hurt and anger. It's not unlike watching a movie. You can feel like you are in the storyline and feel the fear and tension of the movie...until you step outside the theatre and remember you are an observer, the watcher of this story. You can speak for the part of you that feels hurt and sad, saying what it needs. When you don't lead with anger, you'll find it easier to take care of your need yourself or let someone who cares about you help you.

Practicing Mindfulness More Formally

A more formal practice of mindfulness is to sit in stillness with reduced sensory stimulation.

Just close your eyes and sit still or lay down. Notice your breathing, in and out. When you focus on your breath, your mind quiets. Observe what unfolds without judgment or resistance. Thoughts and feelings will come and go. Notice and name them.

This may be difficult without some guidance. Guided meditation induces deep relaxation throughout your body and mind. The practice of Integrative Restoration, or iRest (Miller), or Yoga Nidra, was adapted from the teachings of yogic teachings that are thousands of years old.

The practice of iRest/Yoga Nidra provides guidelines for nonjudgmental Self investigating. This is an in-depth meditative process that helps the brain integrate our different parts, and reconnects us to our deepest, heartfelt desires. Current research supports the positive changes in the brain with the use of Yoga Nidra daily (Nilsson). And it is a guided meditation so all you have to do is take 20 minutes to listen in a relaxed pose.

Used daily, Yoga Nidra builds our mindsight, where we can step into being the observer and participant at the same time. We have sight of what our mind is up to. We can stay aware in our lives and notice before responding. As Self takes leadership, we become more at ease in our life, and our life choices make sense for all of us, not just parts of us. We feel in the flow of life.

Conclusion

Better connections to ourselves lead to more positive connections to others and our world.

My hope for you now is that you are ready to begin to live your life with confidence and choice. You have the ability to choose your response, rather than to react. The family of parts inside of you now acts as advisers who can help you, not cause chaos. Through intention and practice, you can continue to cultivate your Self leadership through calm, compassion, and curiosity.

The most valuable gift you can give yourself is this Self care. Give time to yourself. We give attention and support to ourselves when we remember to breathe, to love, and to sit in stillness with Self. This is what it means to heal from within or to change from within. You heal by using activities that guide you from both the top down (using your thinking brain with the lens of our internal family) and from the bottom up (using the primitive part of your brain and your body).

With your new sense of balanced awareness, you in Self can hear your parts say or shout *I am too tired to work late! I need to seek the comforts of my home!* And you will have the courage to meet that need.

When you hear the voice of shame saying, *People won't like me if I make that decision,* you can soothe that part and get to understand it better. You can find the answer to the question, *Where did this part of me get a belief that people would think bad of it for caring for itself?* You will be able to let go of these old outdated beliefs when your parts feel connected and believe that you have put yourself back in charge. You can now change your "habits" with strength and purpose.

When you do this, when we all do this, we can invite in new stories and new beliefs which will become our new habits. You will have changed your brain and your life.

Yes, you can be better connected with your Self and others authentically, with a richness that will fill your life. Reach out, lean in, and lead from your deepest yearnings in Self leadership. Why not? You now know how to begin.

Works Cited

Begley, Sharon. *Train Your Mind, Change Your Brain: How a New Science Reveals Our Extraordinary Potential to Transform Ourselves.* New York: Ballantine, 2007. Print.

Dipietro, Janet A. "The Role of Prenatal Maternal Stress in Child Development." *Current Directions in Psychological Science* 13.2 (2004): 71-74. Web.

Doidge, Norman, M.D. *The Brain That Changes Itself: Stories of Personal Triumph from the Frontiers of Brain Science.* New York: Viking, 2007. Print.

Eagleman, David. *Incognito*: The Secret Lives of the Brain. New York: Pantheon, 2011. Print.

Frankl, Viktor E., M.D., Ph.D. *Man's Search for Meaning.* Boston: Beacon, 2006. Print.

Goleman, Daniel, Ph.D. *Emotional Intelligence: Why It Can Matter More than IQ.* London: Bloomsbury, 1996. Print.

Huizink, Anja C., Edu J. H. Mulder, and Jan K. Buitelaar. "Prenatal Stress and Risk for Psychopathology: Specific Effects or Induction of General Susceptibility?" *Psychological Bulletin* 130.1 (2004): 115-42. Web.

Miller, Rick. *Yoga Nidra: A Meditative Practice for Deep Relaxation and Healing.* Boulder, CO: Sounds True, 2010. Print.

Neff, Kristin, Ph.D. *Self-Compassion: Stop Beating Yourself up and Leave Insecurity Behind.* New York: William Morrow, 2011. Print.

Nilsson, Robert. "Pictures of the Brain's Activity during Yoga Nidra." *Bindu* 1997: n. pag. *Bindu*. Bindu Publishers. Web. 23 Jan. 2015. <http://www.yogameditation.com/Articles/Issues-of-Bindu/Bindu-11/Pictures-of-the-brain-s-activity-during-Yoga-Nidra>.
Rosenberg, Marshall B., Ph.D. *Nonviolent Communication: A Language of Life*. Encinitas, CA: PuddleDancer, 2003. Print.

Schwartz, Richard C., Ph.D. *Internal Family Systems Therapy*. New York: Guilford, 1995. Print.

Van Der Kolk, Bessel, M.D. *Body Keeps the Score: Brain, Mind, and Body in the Healing of Trauma*. Kindle ed. N.p.: Penguin, 2015.

Beth Rogerson, PhD, LPCC, MFT, Certified IFS Therapist

Beth Rogerson

www.bethrogerson.com

37323727R00031

Made in the USA
Middletown, DE
25 November 2016